strecnology

strecr

Graffix User Manual

...nology

Various Ⓐ Artists

Thames and Hudson

Printed in Slovenia

REM **STRECNOLOGY**

10 REM STRECNOLOGY:
20 REM START:
50 INTRO:
90:

100 REM STRECNOSIS:
110 REM START-UP PROGRAM:
250:

1000 REM STRECNOGRAFFIX:
1010 REM PROGRAM 1:
1500:

2000 REM TECNOLYSIS:
2010 REM PROGRAM 2:
2500:

3000 REM STUDIOACTIVE:
3010 REM PROGRAM 3:
3500:

WP, OP'S: Emma, Cecilia, Glenys, **Marrisa**

Acknowledgement

**ALL THE TUTORS
HND COURSE
FACULTY OF DESIGN AND VISUAL ARTS
STOCKPORT COLLEGE OF FURTHER AND HIGHER
EDUCATION.**

DAVE CURTIS and TABERNACLE

**NEIL JOHNSTON,
ROBERT AUSTIN,
PORTOBELLO TRUST**

**ALEX,LINDA,ANDY,
BUSINESS RESOURCE CENTRE**

CREATIVE TEAM: Mark Jackson, Sandra Belgrave, Ricky Plante, Scott **Minshall,** Paul **Collins** **Nick** Small, Dylan Hawley Andy Greenwood.

CYNTHIA ROSE

IOANNA MARY DAVE

LONDON UNION OF YOUTH CLUBS.

JENNY McNULTY

TYRONE FORBE, T.A.F.C. POWIS PROWLERS.

MUM and DAD and the BOYS and GIRLS from BIG BUX

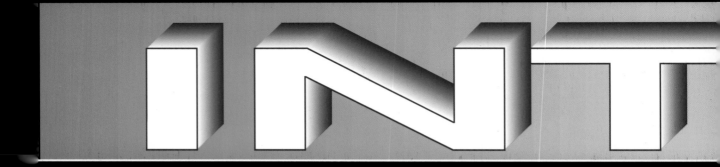

...my name is Mark. Your user-friendly cursor to ...ay's latest design concept, **'STRECNOLOGY'**. ...e technical theory of street graffix.

TRECNOLOGY is a term that fuses the words **'STREET'** and **'TECHNOLOGY'**. This book allows everyone easy **'ACCESS'** to its ideas. The theory and techniques of **STRECNOLOGY** are both explained in its 4-program analysis.

...RECNOSIS: (Start-up program): A theoretical program ...t introduces the user to the basic concepts of ...RECNOLOGY. Its System Structure, Interactive Space ...e Paint Technologies (ISAPT), Visualisation and ...minology.

...RECNOGRAFFIX: (Program 1): A practical program that **'SHOW'**'s the user **'HOW'** to create hand-generated **'ARTICLE'**'s utilizing ISAPT, together with their

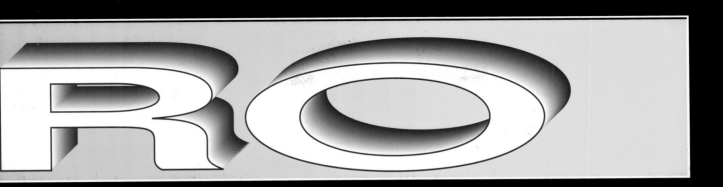

ECNOLYSIS: (Program 2): A functional program
SHOW'ing machine techniques for image generation and
rocessing. Interactive with ISAPT peripherals for
omponent and finished 'ARTICLE's.

STUDIOACTIVE: (Program 3): A business program that
draws on the previous programs to place the theoretical and
technical aspects of **STRECNOLOGY** into viable
commercial applications.

All the programs 'RUN' to and 'FROM' each other. Their
structure is identical, assuming a modular approach and
allowing complete compatibillity when interactive with ISAPT.
Now that you have been 'BOOT STRAPPED', I would like to
wish you, on behalf of Various Artists and myself,

"Happy Programming"

"O.K. Let's Go!!"

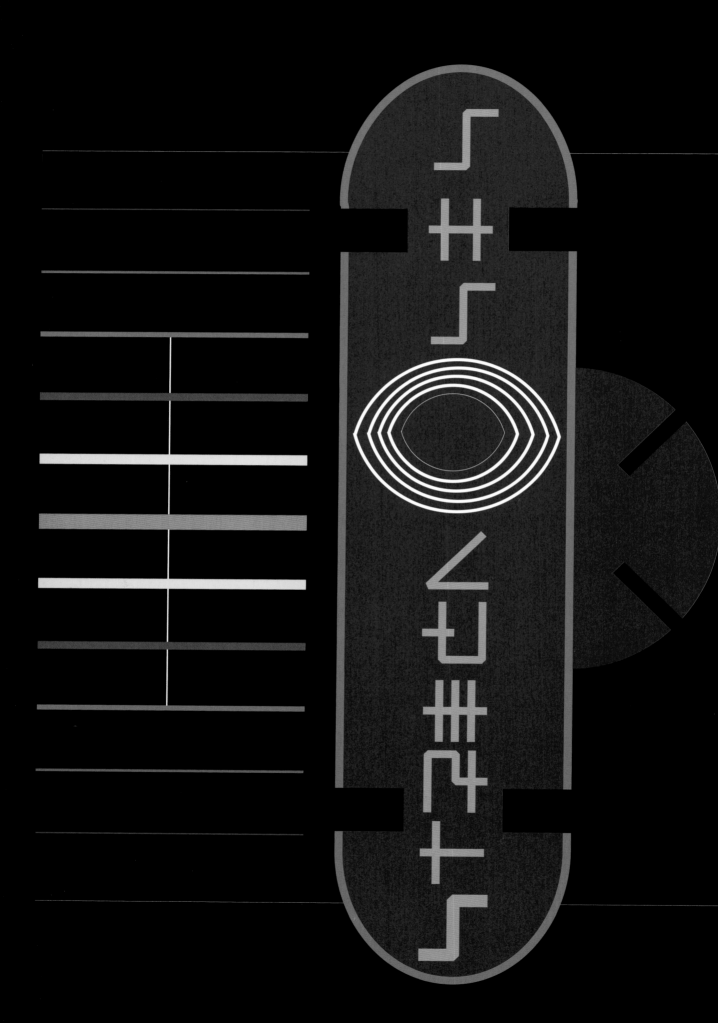

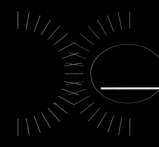

REM **STRECNOSIS**

The program you are about to 'READ' is an analysis of the ideas behind **Strecnology.**

It is a theoretical program that introduces the user to the basic concepts . 'LET'ing the user 'ACCESS' key information on the theory of **Strecnology.**

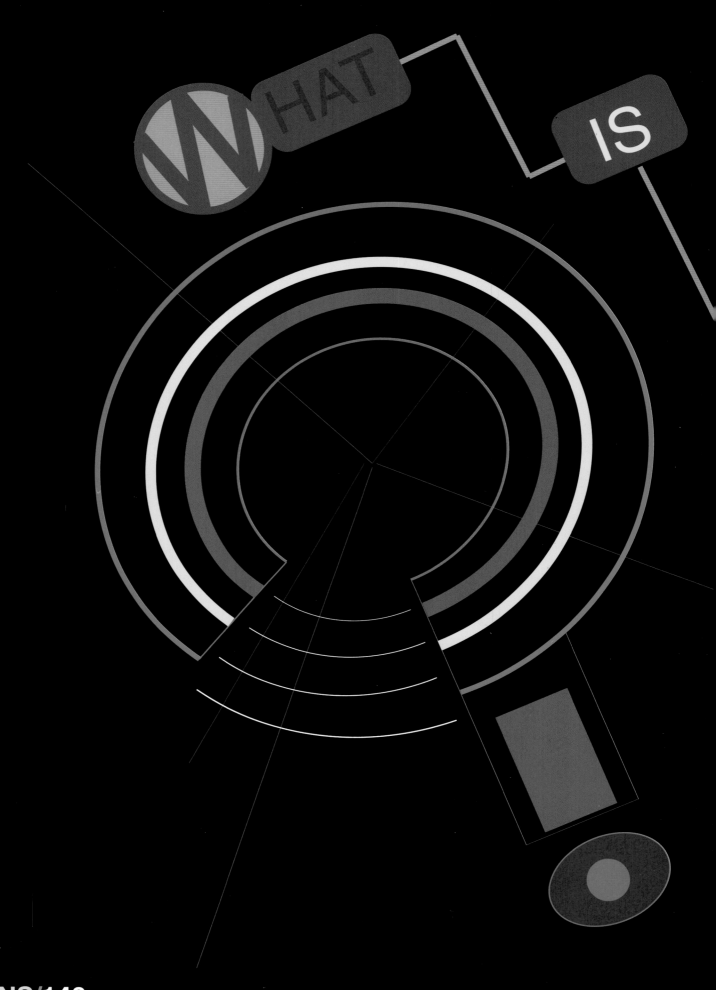

WHAT IS

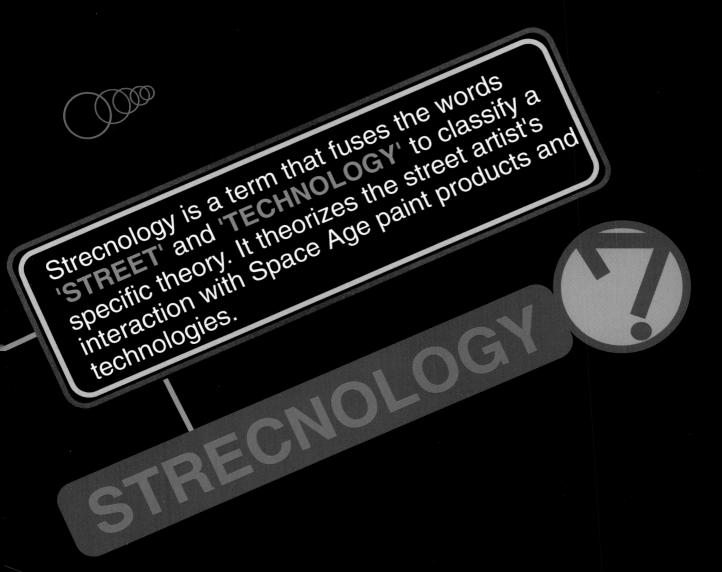

Strecnology is a term that fuses the words 'STREET' and 'TECHNOLOGY' to classify a specific theory. It theorizes the street artist's interaction with Space Age paint products and technologies.

STRECNOLOGY

The term is then applied to the works of artists who create in this field. All the artist has to do to create **Strecnology** is to apply the theory of **Strecnology** to his or her own ideas.

To apply the theory of **Strecnology** the artist must be programmed to understand its System Structure and the meaning of Space Age Paint Technologies; to become fluent in its Terminology; and to have a complete awareness of the style, content and techniques of **Strecnology**. This programming can only be achieved by 'READ'ing this user manual.

THE SYSTEM STRUCTURE OF STRECNOLOGY

In these HI-TEC times any person with a basic knowledge of computers can make the simple analogy between the computer's central processing unit (CPU) and the brain.

If we start by making this analogy, then what do we understand by 'hardware', 'software' and 'peripherals'?

In **Strecnology** the principle of the CPU/brain analogy has been widened to incorporate:

HARDWARE: The physical capacity to generate **Strecnology**.

SOFTWARE: The information that stimulates the hardware in its generation of **Strecnology.**

PERIPHERALS: Space Age Paints and Technologies used to generate component and finished 'ARTICLE's.

By following these basic principles the user will gain a clear understanding of the System Structure of **Strecnology.**

SNS/160

Flow chart for the System Design of the generation of Strecnological 'ARTICLE's.

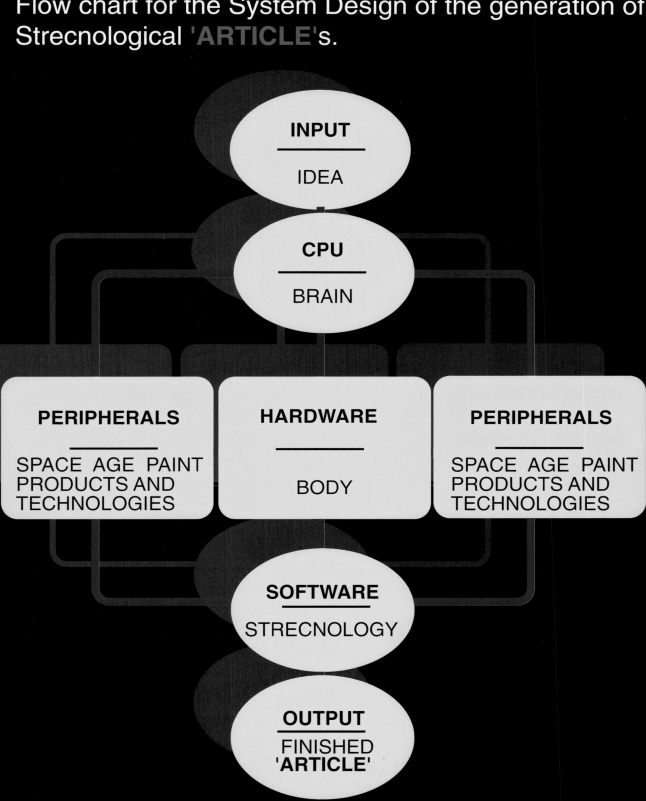

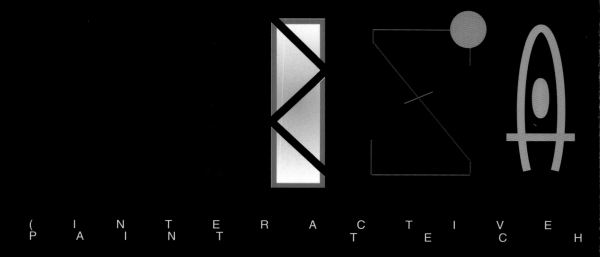

Of all the things that have made an impact on human technological advancement through time, the journey into space provides us with the most profound and universal yet.

So many of the products that surround us and that we take for granted in our everyday lives - from tin foil to training shoes, from CDs to satellite TV - have come about through our efforts to go where no one has gone before.

It seems strange that so little attention is paid to the amount of artist's materials that can be 'ADDRESS'ed under this category. Spray Cans, fibre-tipped pens, correction fluid and instant lettering are all born of this age, but are often dismissed when compared to the traditional artist's materials of oil paint,charcoal and pastels. Why is this, given that the majority of young people born into the space age turn naturally to the materials of their time?

also seems strange that there is so little recognition
f the creative interaction that these young people
ave with their technological surroundings. Office
echnology, fax machines, photocopiers and
omputers - these are dull, routine or repetitive
TASK's, but they can also be transformed into
reative tools or paint boxes without a university
egree in creative technology.

Here is where the 'BASIC's of **Strecnology** lie: the
nteraction of the user's own hardware with ISAPT
eripherals and the software that programs the user
s hardware.

Visualisation

The visuals 'SHOW'n in this manual were completed over a period of 6 years, taking influences from Dadaism, Surrealism, Pop Art and Anglo-American street culture. Various Artists have 'PROCESS'ed their ideas and imagery via ISAPT peripherals to 'DEFINE' a creative 'FORM' visually representative of the theory and techniques of **Strecnology**.

This user manual has been devised by Various Artists to 'LET' the user see 'HOW' the whole concept of Strecnology can be integrated into a complete design 'FORMAT' that reflects our HI-TEC world by 'SHOW'ing chapters as programs and contents as menus. In the colour-coded text, red indicates a command; blue a window or screen; yellow a program name; and green any other key terms.

The concept of **Strecnology** is rooted in a world of computers and space age technology. Therefore its terminology reflects that world. The majority of its terms are based on commands used in the computer language called 'BASIC'. They are appropriate because they express the same or similar value when applied in **Strecnology**. For example, the 'DRAW' command in 'BASIC' means exactly what it says.It allows the user to draw. In **Strecnology** the term 'DRAW'n also means exactly what it says - that the visual instruction has been 'DRAW'n.

Other terms are taken from the music industry, especially engineering terminologies such as 'CUT', 'SCRATCH' and 'BREAK'. Others are borrowed from design terminologies, including 'CAMPAIGN', 'PIECE' and 'LOGO'.

When these terms are integrated into written English they become what is known as PSEUDO CODE. In Strecnology, the PSEUDO CODE is termed TECNOBASIC. TECNOBASIC enables the user to become friendly with ISAPT peripherals.

There are 75 command terms utilized in **Strecnology**

ACCENT
ACCESS
ACROSS
ACTIVATE
ADDRESS
ALLOW
APPLY
ARTICLE

BASIC
BREAK
BUILD

CAMPAIGN
CLEAR
CREATE
CUT

DECAY
DEDICATE
DISK
DRAW

EDIT
ELEMENT
ENLARGE
ENTER
EXAMPLE

FAX
FILL IN
FINISH
FIT
FLAT
FORM
FORMAT
FRAME
FROM
FURNISH

GARNISH

HOLD
HOW

IN FIELD
INPUT

LET
LINE
LOGO

MIX
MODE
MULTI

NEXT

OVER
OUTPUT

PAPER
PASTE
PIECE
PIXEL
PLAY
PORTRAIT
PRINT
PROFILE

RAW
READ
RE-MIX
REPEAT
REVEAL
RUN

SAMPLE
SCAN
SCRATCH
SELECT
SET
SHOW
START

TAG
TASK
TELL
TRACE
TRACK
TUNE

ULTIMATE

VIEW

REM **STRECNOGRAFFIX:** ⟵─────────────────────────

1010 REM PROGRAM 1: MENU:
1020 INTRO:
1030 DATA:
1040 DATA: **INT** / WINDOW *1:
1050 DATA: **INT** / WINDOW *2:
1090:

sTrecno

1100 REM   **TYPOGRAFFIX:**
1110 DATA: **TYP** / WINDOW*1:
1120 DATA: **TYP** / WINDOW*2:
1130 DATA: **TYP** / WINDOW*3:
1140 TYP / SCREEN*1:
1190:

1200 REM   SRECNOPAINT:
1210 DATA:
1220 DATA: **STP / WINDOW*1/*2:**
1230 DATA: **STP / WINDOW*3/*4:**
1240 STP / SCREEN*1:
1290:

graffi>x

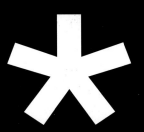

1300 REM   HI - STYLE:
1310 DATA:
1320 HST / WINDOW*1:
1330 HST / WINDOW*2:
1340 HST / SCREEN*1:
1390:

In this first program we 'ACCESS' the user-generated science of **STRECNOGRAFFIX.** It is a practical program that contains 3 sub-routines : **TYPOGRAFFIX** , **STRECNOPAINT** and **HI-STYLE.** These practical 'INPUT' routines 'LET' the user 'OUTPUT' 'ARTICLES'. They also 'TELL' the user about ISAPT products and presentation techniques for the completion of user-defined 'ARTICLES'. In **TYPOGRAFFIX** , the user will 'ACCESS' information on typograffik generation, on composition and on computer-generated techniques.

STRECNOPAINT 'SHOW''s the user how to apply
the products and tecnomixes. These are the
reproduction and presentation techniques of ISAPT.

HI - STYLE is a 'PROFILE' of various Artists' own
cellulose paint application. It 'LET's the user 'ACCESS'
the abstract qualities of cellulose paint, so allowing the
user to define the indefinable.

INT / WINDOW*2:

By 'RUN'ing this program, you will become user-friendly

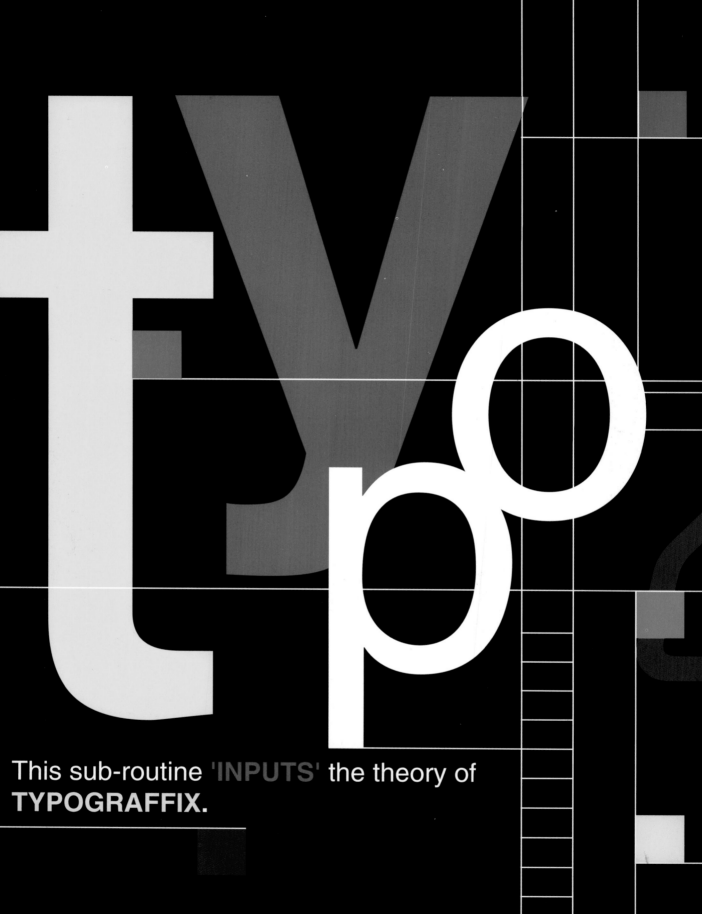

This sub-routine 'INPUTS' the theory of
TYPOGRAFFIX.

It involves the 'SAMPLE'ing of **typograffik** characters and their re-composition into user-defined **typograffik** 'SET's. The objective is to create a **typograffik** user-personality.

The user must first define an identity. In this program Various Artists have 'EXAMPLE'd the user-personality 'A1 GRAFIKZ'

Secondly, the user 'SAMPLE's a style made of **typograffik** characters or lettering. These styles can be 'SAMPLE'd from any source. The 'A1' from the 'EXAMPLE' has been 'SAMPLE'd from an instant lettering catalogue. The word 'GRAFFIX' has been hand - generated.

RaFFiX

Thirdly, the user is required to 'FURNISH' or 'GARNISH' the character/s with any embellishment that re-inforces the user-personality of the chosen style.

Once the separate elements of **TYPOGRAFFIX** have been defined, you can then 'RUN' them through your own style-processor to 'BUILD' a 'FINISH'ed user-personality.

TYP / WINDOW*1: 'SHOW's the user how to create a 'SET'.

TYP / WINDOW*1:

The term 'SET' is applied to the composition of **typograffik** 'ELEMENT's. In this 'SET' we have all the **typograffik** 'ELEMENT's that have been run through the user's own style-processor to define a user-personality. The 'SET' is presented with a monochrome 'FILL IN'.

TYP / **WINDOW*2**

In **TYP** / **SCREEN** *1: we 'VIEW' a HI-RES 'SET'. It is presented 'IN FIELD' with a two-colour 'FORMAT', a hand-generated outline with a computer-generated 'FILL-IN'.

TYP / 1140

You are now 'ENTER'ing **STRECNOPAINT**. The application of ISAPT products and their tecnomixes. The reproduction and presentation techniques for the generation of user-defined graffik 'ARTICLE's.

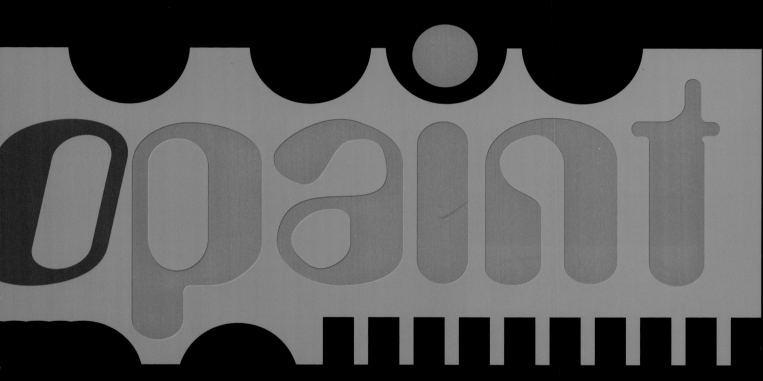

The program 'SHOW's 'EXAMPLE's of the generation of 'LINE' styles, 'FILL IN' applications and reproduction techniques.

STRECNOLOGY

STP / WINDOW * 1: features 'TAG DRAW'n - a user-defined 'LINE' style.'DRAW'n in monochrome by fibre-tipped pen. The 'ARTICLE' has then been reproduced by laser copier, with operation in SPOT COLOUR 'MODE'.

STP / WINDOW*2:

To generate the 'ARTICLE' 'SHOW'n in **STP** / WINDOW*2: the user must first create a black / white outline graffik. After utilizing a colour marker 'FILL IN', the 'RAW' 'ARTICLE' can then be reproduced by a laser copier as a CLIENT PRESENTATION VISUAL.

STP/ WINDOW*3:
'SHOW's a user-defined
'ARTICLE', utilizing an
ISAPT tecnomix of
permanent marker and
cellulose paint.

STP / WINDOW*4: 'SHOW's a user-defined **'ARTICLE'** th
utilizes cellulose paint application to generate a
background. The character is **'TRACE'**d on the backgroun
and an **ISAPT** tecnomix of enamel paint and permanent
marker is used to generate the character **'FILL IN'**.

STP / SCREEN*1: features a finished **'ARTICLE'**
constructed of **'TAG DRAW'** and **BLACK 'LINE'** stylizatio
utilizing an **ISAPT** tecnomix **'FILL IN'** of permanent marke

STP / 1240

Welcome to **HI-STYLE**. A 'PROFILE' of Various Artists' own cellulose paint routine.

In this routine, Various Artists have chosen to 'VIEW' the abstract qualities of cellulose paint that has been applied to a surface by Spray Can. These instruments use compressed air to atomise paint and apply it to a surface in a fine spray. You can apply flat or graded tones, thin or fat lines to create your 'PIECE'.

There are no pre-set techniques. By experimenting, users learn and discover their own techniques to produce a style that can be defined as HI-STYLE.

HST / 1340

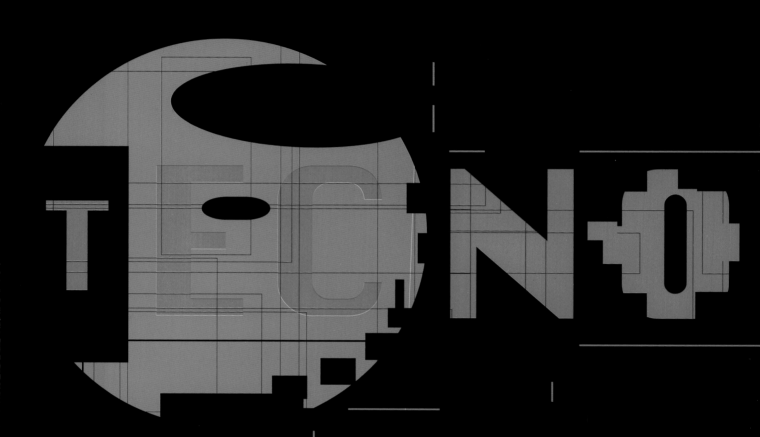

REM **TECNOLYSIS**

2010 REM **PROGRAM 2: MENU:**
2020 **INTRO:**
2040 **DATA: INT/WINDOW *1/*2:**
2050 **DATA: INT/WINDOW *3:**
2090 **:**

2100 REM **SCRATCHTECNIK:**
2120 **DATA: SCK/WINDOW *1/*2:**
2130 **DATA: SCK/WINDOW *3:**
2140 **SCK/SCREEN *1:**
2190 **:**

2200 REM **PHOTOACTIVE:**
2220 **DATA: PTA/WINDOW *1:**
2230 **DATA: PTA/WINDOW *2:**
2240 **PTA/SCREEN *1:**
2290 **:**

2300 REM **IMPLIED MOTION:**
2320 **DATA: IPM/WINDOW *1:**
2330 **DATA: IPM/WINDOW *2:**
2340 **IPM/SCREEN *1:**
2390 **:**

STRECNOLOGY

Your user 'INPUT' channel control is now receiving
TECNOLYSIS - a functional program 'TUNE'd for the
development of user-defined generation and
machine-interaction techniques.

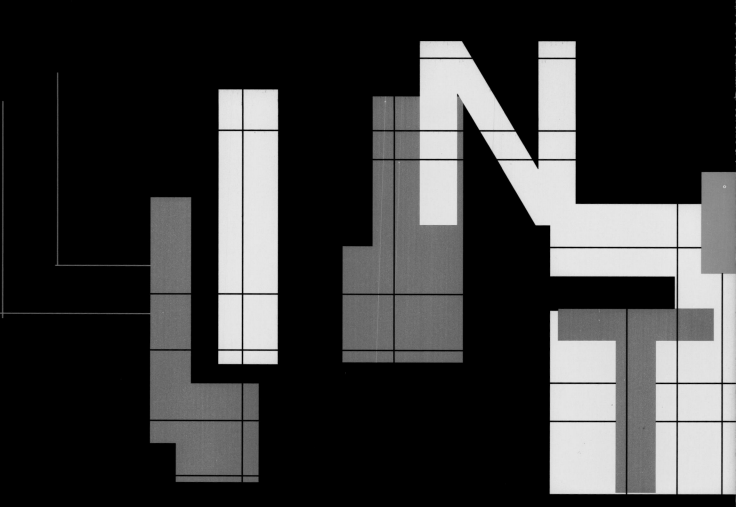

As a functional program, it 'EXAMPLE's techniques that
are interactive with the ISAPT peripherals - photocopier,
fax machine and computer scanner - for image generation and processing. These 'OUTPUT' devices can be
manipulated by two methods: user-defined generation
and user machine-interaction.

User machine-interaction can be 'ACCESS'ed wher
user exploits the operating system of ISAPT peripheral
generate textural, tonal or presentation techniques for u
defined 'ARTICLE's. The user can 'READ' the generat
techniques in the sub-routine, PHOTOACTIVE.

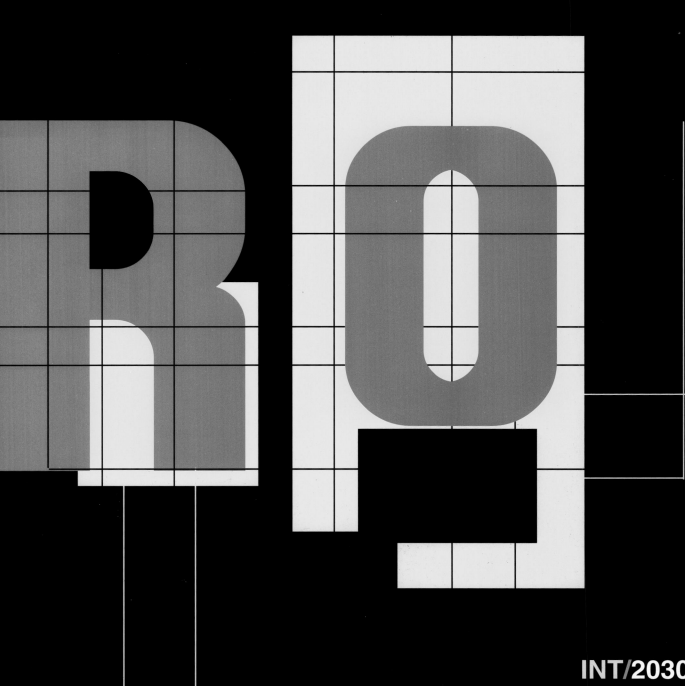

STRECNOLOGY

INT/WINDOW*1:

SCRATCHTECNIK:

'REVEAL's to the user 'HOW' to develop the basic technique of **TECNOLYSIS:** the 'SCRATCH'. You see 'HOW' to 'ACCESS' the photocopier as a visual mixing desk, as well as alternative 'SCRATCH' presentation techniques.

INT/WINDOW*2:

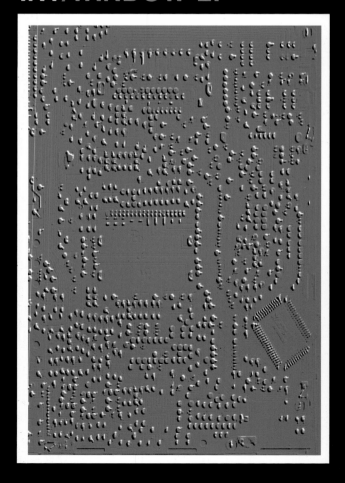

PHOTOACTIVE: 'SHOW's the technological manipulation of three-dimensional objects when captured in a two-dimensional 'FRAME', together with the generation of applied textural values.

INT/WINDOW*3:

IMPLIED MOTION:
Applies 'MULTI-TRACK' ing techniques to 'SAMPLE'd images to generate 'EXAMPLE's of static animation.

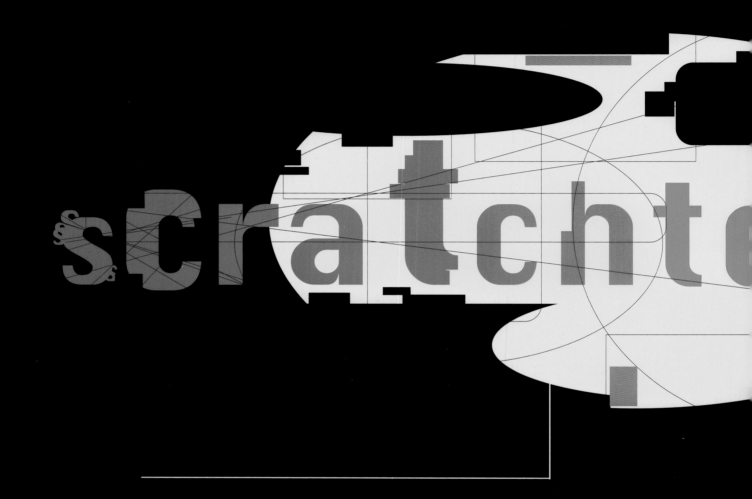

The principal 'ISAPT' peripheral is an 'OUTPUT' device: the photocopier. It is on this peripheral that the theory of TECNOLYSIS is based. 'SCRATCH' is the basic technique of TECNOLYSIS.

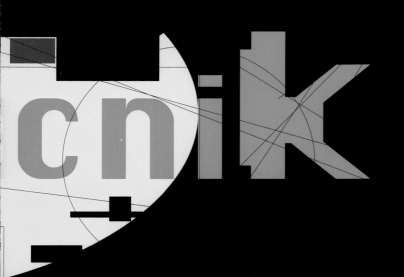

To create a 'SCRATCH' technique, the user must 'START' with a 'SAMPLE'd image. The image can be 'SAMPLE'd from any source. Next the user must 'ACCESS' a photocopier to generate the 'SCRATCH' technique.

The user must 'PLAY' the 'SAMPLE' d image by utilizing various degrees of hand movement 'OVER' or 'ACROSS' the light bar as it moves under the glass screen of the photocopier. This will then produce a 'SCRATCH'ed image. It is up to the user to define the outcome and style of the 'SCRATCH'ed image, 'REPEAT'ing the process until a user-defined style is achieved.

STRECNOLOGY

SCK/WINDOW*1/*2:

SCK/2120

In **SCK**/WINDOW*1: A photograph of a woman's face is 'SELECT'ed to be 'SAMPLE'd. The 'SAMPLE'd image can then be 'SCRATCH'ed. This is achieved by placing the image face down in a pre-selected position on the glass screen of a photocopier. The user then 'PLAY's the image by moving the hand in a rhythmic motion back and forth across the light bar of the copier as it repro-duces the image. This is user-defined generation.

The 'SAMPLE'd and 'SCRATCH'ed image is represented in monochrome, 'SHOW'ing the textural value of the image reproduced by photocopier.

The 'ARTICLE' 'SHOW'n in **SCK**/WINDOW*2: is a 'SAMPLE'**d,** 'SCRATCH'ed and 'FAX'ed image.

A photograph of a face was 'SELECT'ed to be 'SAMPLE'd. This 'SAMPLE'd image was then 'SCRATCH'ed on a photocopier. Once user-defined generation was complete, the image was then reproduced by a fax machine 'SHOW'ing the tonal value of 'FAX'.

'n **SCK**/WINDOW*3: an image was 'SELECT'ed for 'SAMPLE'ing because of its original, tabloid, half-tone value. The 'SAMPLE'd image was 'ENLARGE'd by photocopier to fit a user-defined 'FORMAT'.

A user-defined 'SCRATCH' technique was applied to the 'FORMAT'ed, 'SAMPLE'd mage. 'NEXT' the image was reproduced with an applied 'DECAY' technique. 'DECAY' is

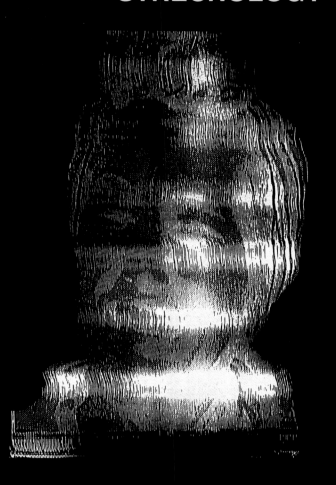

SCK/WINDOW*3

a result of 'PRINT'ing image 'FROM' image - 'RUN'ning off a single print from the previous print on the photocopier to achieve a 'DECAY' quality of image.
This image 'HOLD's a 'DECAY' value of minus 15 (dec:15-) on a scale of -1 (copy) to i (infinity). The 'FINISH'd image is reproduced by laser copier operating in REVERSE 'MODE'.

SCK/SCREEN*1: 'SHOW's a 'SELECT'ed, 'SAMPLE'd and 'SCRATCH'ed image. Reproduced by laser copier operating in SPOT COLOUR 'MODE' to produce a finished 'MIX'ed 'ARTICLE'.

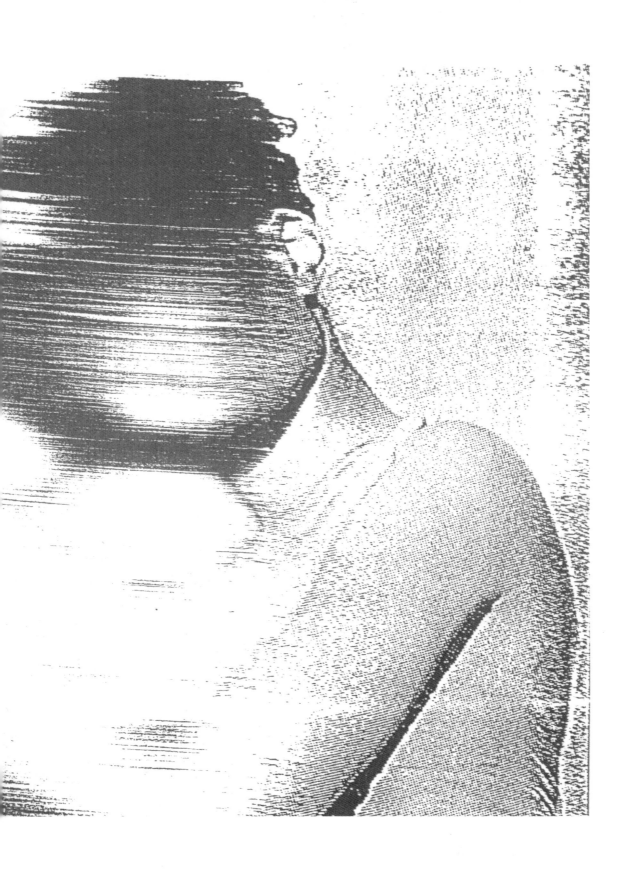

PHOTOACTIVE is the technical manipulation of a three-dimensional object that has been 'FORMAT'ed into a two-dimensional 'FRAME' utilizing user machine-interaction. This 'LET's the user exploit the operating system of ISAPT peripherals to produce textural and tonal values.

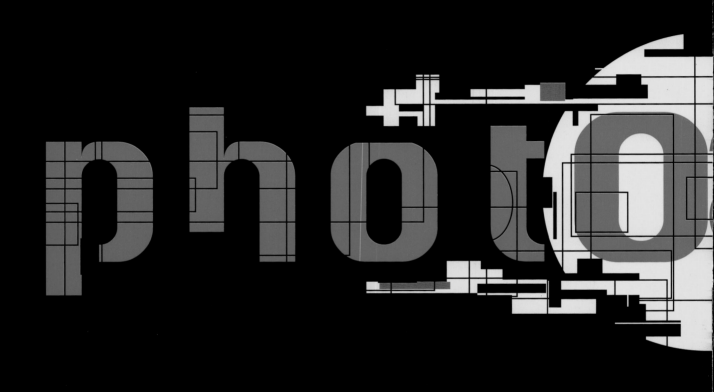

To generate a **PHOTOACTIVE** 'ARTICLE' the user must 'SAMPLE' a three-dimensional object. The user must then process the object via an ISAPT peripheral to produce a two-dimensional representation. The user may process the 'SAMPLE'd object by employing the user's own defined 'SCRATCH' techniques.

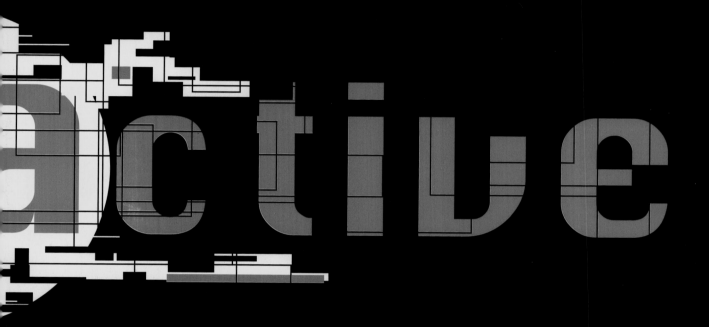

active

User machine-interaction comes 'NEXT'. This interaction is co-defined by the user and by the peripherals' own reproduction apparatus. When the user has employed these techniques and 'SELECT'ed a 'RAW' 'ARTICLE', he or she may 'EDIT', then employ a laser copier in 'MODE' to produce a 'FINISH'ed 'ARTICLE'.

STRECNOLOGY

PTA/WINDOW*1: 'SHOW's a calculator as a **PHOTOACTIVE** 'ARTICLE'. The calculator was placed face down on to the glass screen of a photocopier. The lid of the photocopier was placed over the calculator and a 'PRINT' was taken. Because of the three-dimensional status of the calculator, the lid of the copier did not close flat.

PTA/WINDOW*1:

This 'ALLOW'ed the three-dimensional object to cast a shadow, so creating a tonal value. To 'ACCENT'uate the value a second 'PRINT' was taken with the copier's contrast control at maximum darkness. This end 'PRINT' was reproduced by laser copier, operating in REVERSE, in EXTRA BLACK 'MODE'.

PTA/WINDOW*2: 'SHOW's a slice of bread as a **PHOTOACTIVE** 'ARTICLE'. To generate this **PHOTOACTIVE** 'ARTICLE', the slice of bread was 'SCAN'ned by computer scanner. Once 'SCAN'ned into the computer, the image can be manipulated.

PTA/2220

In this 'ARTICLE', the image has been 'COLORIZED', an 'EXAMPLE' of user machine-interaction.

The image has then been 'PRINT'ed by laser printer and presented in full colour to 'SHOW' the tonal and textural value. This is an 'EXAMPLE' of how to turn white bread into toast without putting it under the grill.

PTA/WINDOW*2:

PTA/SCREEN*1: 'SHOW's a soft drinks container as a **PHOTOACTIVE** 'ARTICLE' presented as a full 'MIX'ed 'TRACK'. To generate this **PHOTOACTIVE** 'ARTICLE', the container was first rolled in parallel motion with the light bar of the photocopier to create a two-dimensional 'ARTICLE'. This 'ARTICLE' was then 'SCRATCH'ed. Then, to produce the full 'MIX'ed 'TRACK' presentation, two 'SCRATCH'ed images were taken from the 'ARTICLE' and 'PRINT'ed on 'ACETATE' as 'CLEAR' images. These images were placed together and a single image was 'PRINT'ed off.

The resulting image was then reproduced by laser copier operating in SPOT COLOUR 'MODE'.

PTA/2240

IMPLIED MOTION is an experiment in the production of movement. This is achieved by utilizing user-defined 'SCRATCH' techniques with 'MULTI-TRACK'ing to create 'EXAMPLE' 'ARTICLE's of static animation.

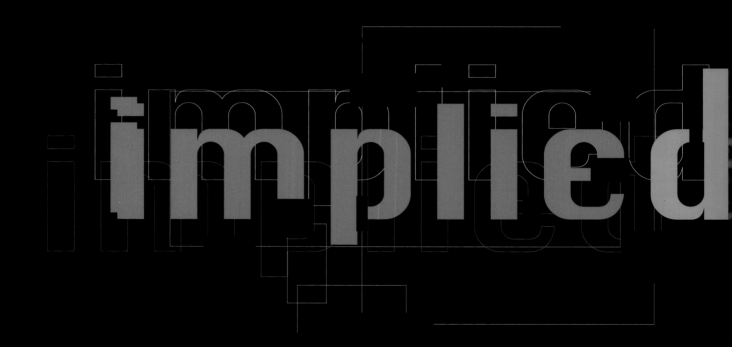

To generate **IMPLIED MOTION**, the user must 'SAMPLE' and define an image to be animated. The user may then utilize his or her own user-defined 'SCRATCH' techniques to generate movement. To accentuate this movement the user may use 'MULTI-TRACK'ing techniques.

MULTI-TRACK'ing can be achieved by reproducing images onto a 'CLEAR' surface, e.g. acetate, then 'PRINT'ing from two or more images to produce one 'FLAT' image.
To make 'MULTI-TRACK'ing simpler, the user must have an understanding of the 'PRINT'ing process of a colour photocopier.

The colour copier 'PRINT's in a specific three-colour sequence: Yellow, Cyan, Magenta (yellow, blue, red). These three colours are called primary colours and when mixed together they create all other colours except white. White is provided by the paper; laser copiers have an EXTRA BLACK 'MODE'.

By 'CLEAR' 'PRINT'ing and by manipulating the colour printing process, the user can define his or her own 'MULTI-TRACK'ing techniques.

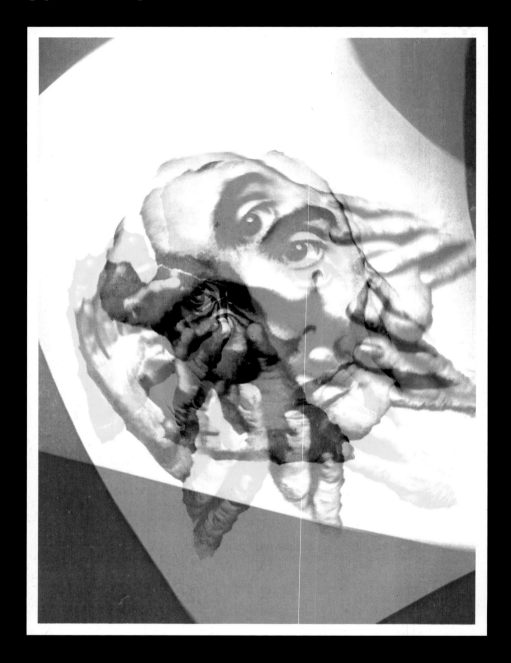

IPM/WINDOW*1:

An image was 'SELECT'ed for 'SAMPLE' ing. This image was then 'MULTI-TRACE'd on a colour copier. Utilizing the colour 'PRINT' process the image was turned as each colour was 'PRINT'ed, 'SHOW' ing a circular motion.

IPM/WINDOW*2: 'SHOW's a user-generated image that has been 'MULTI-TRACK'ed to 'SHOW' a 'BREAK' movement. An image was defined by 'SAMPLE'ing a number of 'SELECT'ed images for generation. This user-defined generation was 'MULTI-TRACK'ed on a colour copier. Utilizing the colour 'PRINT' process, the image was moved to the right as each colour was 'PRINT'ed.

IPM/WINDOW*2:

IPM/SCREEN*1: 'SHOW's a full colour 'MIX'ed 'TRACK'. An image was 'SELECT'ed for 'SAMPLE'ing because of its textural value. This 'SAMPLE'd image was 'SCRATCH'ed on a black and white photocopier. The monochrome 'SCRATCH'ed image was 'MULTI-TRACK'ed on a colour copier. Utilizing the colour 'PRINT' process, the monochrome 'SCRATCH' image was then transferred to a 'CLEAR' TRACK. The 'CLEAR' 'TRACK' was placed over the 'MULTI-TRACK'ed image and reproduced by laser copier to produce a 'FINISH'ed, 'MULTI-TRACK'ed image.

IMP/2340

stüdio

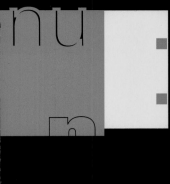

REM **STUDIOACTIVE**

3010 REM PROGRAM
3020 INTRO:
3040 DATA: INT/WIND
3050 DATA: INT/WIND
3090 :

3100 REM **LOGOPRO**
3120 DATA: **LGP/WINI**
3130 DATA: **LGP/WINI**
3190 :

3200 REM DEDIART:
3220 DATA: **DDA/WIN**
3230 DATA: **DDA/WIN**
3240 DDA/SCREEN *1
3290 :

3300 REM ARTVERTIS
3320 AVT/SCREEN *1
3340 DATA: AVT/WINI
3350 DATA: AVT/WINI
3360 AVT/SCREEN *2
3390 :

Re-tune 'CHANNEL's for **STUDIOACTIVE.**

tro

Program 3 'SHOW's how
finished '**ARTICLE**'s into c
applications. As a business
three sub-routines. **LOGO**
and **ARTVERTISING**. The
routines '**LET**' the user '**AC**

STRECNOLOGY

In LOGOPROM: the user will be 'SHOW'n examples of 'HOW' to 'APPLY' a user-defined 'SET' as a 'LOGO' identity for a Graffik design studio. Desk Top Publishing (DTP) software and a computer scanner are used. The 'SET' has been applied to stationery and promotional materials.

INT/WINDOW*1:

I'M SURE CAROLYN'S JUST TRYING TO AVOID SEX. I'M GOING TO STAY AWAKE UNTIL SHE COMES TO BED

DEDIART: 'SHOW's the user 'HOW' to 'DEDICATE' finished 'ARTICLE's to 'EXAMPLE'd commercial applications. It also 'REVEAL's optional 'PAINT' techniques.

INT/3040

ARTVERTISING is a 'PROFILE' of Various Artists' own brand of advertising. It 'SHOW's the Various Artists' own advertising 'CAMPAIGN' promoting their image-regeneration service.

FIND OUT WHAT IT'S LIKE TO BE A MODEL.

INT/WINDOW*2:

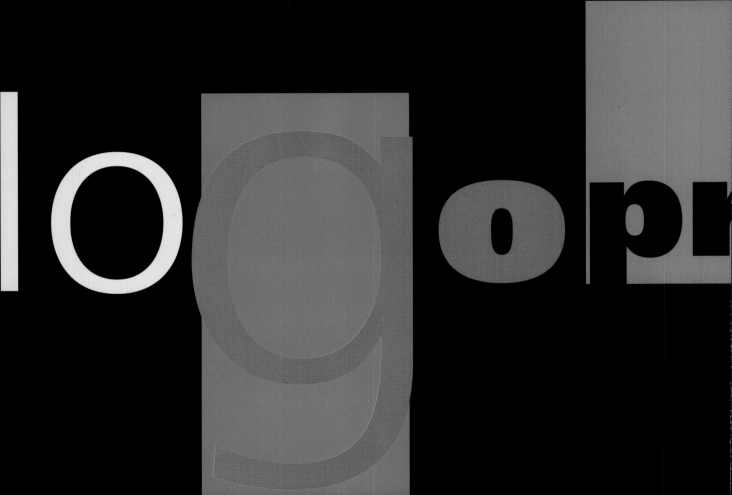

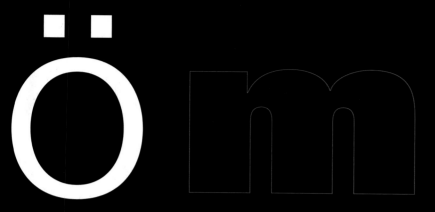

Öm

This sub-routine 'SHOW's 'HOW' to 'APPLY' a user-defined 'SET' as a logo to promote a Graffik design studio. The 'SET' has been applied to the studio's own stationery and promotional material. To utilize **LOGOPROM** to its 'ULTIMATE' the user must first 'CREATE' a user-defined 'SET' as shown in the **TYPOGRAFFIX** sub-routine from the **STRECNOGRAFFIX** program.

'NEXT' the user should 'ACCESS' a computer with the most advanced Desk Top Publishing software and a scanner - a machine that can scan an image into a computer memory.

If the user cannot 'ACCESS' a computer, then the traditional artwork method called 'PASTE' up could be employed. This method consists of 'PASTE'ing all elements of the design onto stiff card to 'FORM' the artwork to be sent to the printers.

STRECNOLOGY

In **LGP**/WINDOW*1: The 'SET' has been applied to a business card 'FORMAT'. This was achieved by 'SCAN'ing the 'SET' into the computer. 'NEXT', utilizing the DTP software, a business card 'FORMAT' was 'CREATE'd. The 'SCAN'ed 'SET' was then retrieved from the computer's memory and applied to the card 'FORMAT' along with the studio address, telephone number and fax numbers.

LGP/WINDOW*1:

tel:010 45 78 33
fax:010 45 07 12

directors: I moncrief CDM
reg no.FA09359A

the terminal
damstraat 20
amsterdam
ZIP 251272

LGP/WINDOW*2:

In **LGP**/WINDOW*2: The 'SET' has been applied to a sticker 'FORMAT' to advertise the design studio. Again, the same method is used. All artwork can be stored on 'DISK' to take to a printer for large 'PRINT RUN's.

tel:010 45 78 33
fax:010 45 07 12

the terminal
damstraat 20
amsterdam
ZIP 251272

directors: I moncrief CDM
reg no.FA09359A

In **LGP**/WINDOW*3: The 'SET' has been applied to a letterhead'FORMAT'   Production is identical to that of the business card. The letterhead can be 'PRINT'ed individua off the computer's own printer.

This sub-routine 'SHOW's 'ARTICLE's that have
been 'CREATE'd by applying the concepts and
techniques of **Strecnology.** Users are then
'SHOW'n various market applications for user-
defined styles. When these market applications
are 'REVEAL'ed users will be able to
'DEDICATE' their defined styles

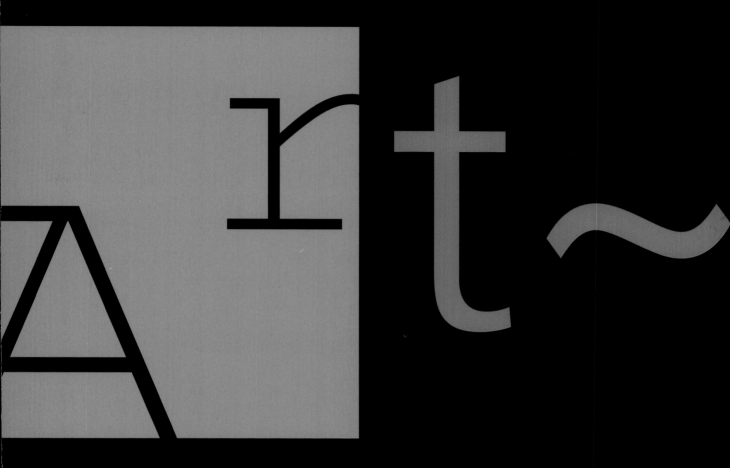

The user is introduced to the Heat Transfer Process, by which an image is transferred in 'REVERSE' onto a special 'PAPER' by laser copier. This 'PAPER' can then be placed onto a garment,such as a cotton T-shirt or denim jacket, and the image is then transferred onto the cloth by applying heat. In this case a Heat Press applied to the 'PAPER' produces a washable 'PRINT'.

In **DDA**/WINDOW*1: An 'ARTICLE' has been 'CREATE'd by 'APPLY'ing the theory of **TECNOLYSIS.** The chosen market application for this 'DEDICATE'd 'ARTICLE' is publication in quantity as an A3 poster by colour laser copier.

DDA/WINDOW*1:

In **DDA**/WINDOW*2: An 'ARTICLE' has been 'CREATE'd by 'APPLY'ing the theory of **TECNOLYSIS and STRECNOPAINT.** As a 'DEDICATE'd 'ARTICLE', its chosen market application is publication as a designer 'PRINT'.

DDA/WINDOW*2:

DDA/3220

In **DDA**/**WINDOW*3:** An 'ARTICLE' has been 'CREATE'd by 'APPLY'ing the theory of **STRECNOPAINT.** The chosen market application for this 'DEDICATE'd 'ARTICLE' involves 'ACCESS' to the Heat Transfer Process for publication as a T-shirt 'PRINT'.

DDA/**WINDOW*3:**

DDA/**WINDOW*4:**

In **DDA**/**WINDOW*4:** An 'ARTICLE' has been 'CREATE'd by 'APPLY'ing the theory of **TECNOLYSIS** and **STRECNOPAINT.** A black and white photocopy taken from a photograph has been coloured. The 'ARTICLE' has then been reproduced by colour laser copier to 'FIT' a 'PORTRAIT' picture 'FRAME' - its commercial application.

DDA/3240

The 'ARTICLE's shown in DDA/SCREEN*1: Have been 'SAMPLE'd from newspapers and coloured according to the theory of Strecnopaint. The 'ARTICLE's have been individually reproduced by laser copier for commercial application as a set of postcards on a single theme.

ÄErtv

rt i$in g*

As a creative routine it 'SHOW's the user 'HOW'
to generate creative advertising by 'SAMPLE'ing
existing advertising images and 'PROCESS'ing
the images via the theory and techniques of
Strecnology.

AVT/3320

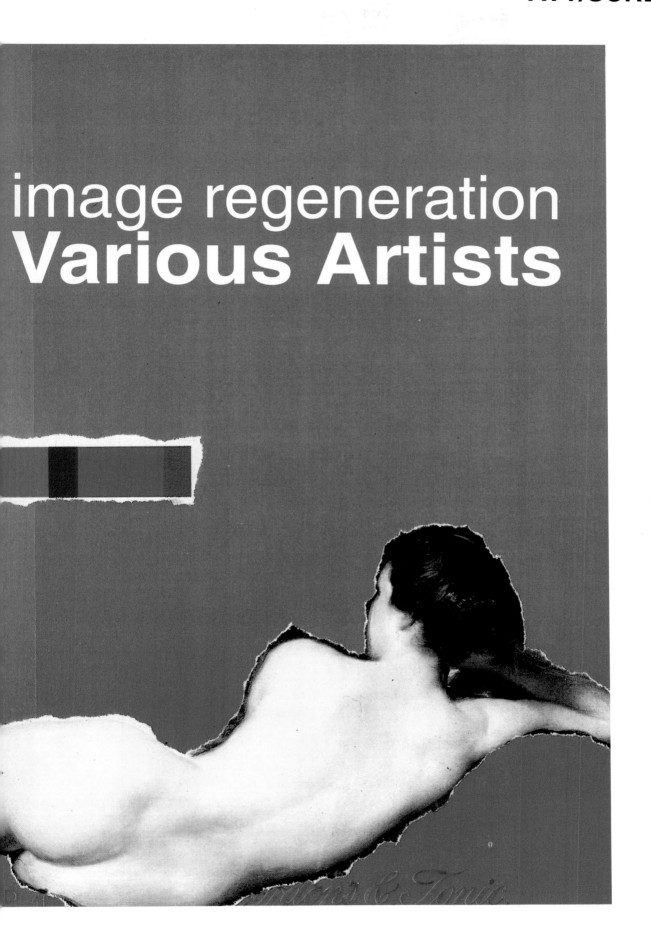

image regeneration
Various Artists

AVT/WINDOW*1:

AVT/WINDOW*1: 'SHOW's a 'RE-MIX' image operating in 'MODE'.

AVT/WINDOW*2: 'SHOW's an 'APPLY'ed 'SCRATCH' technique for image regeneration.

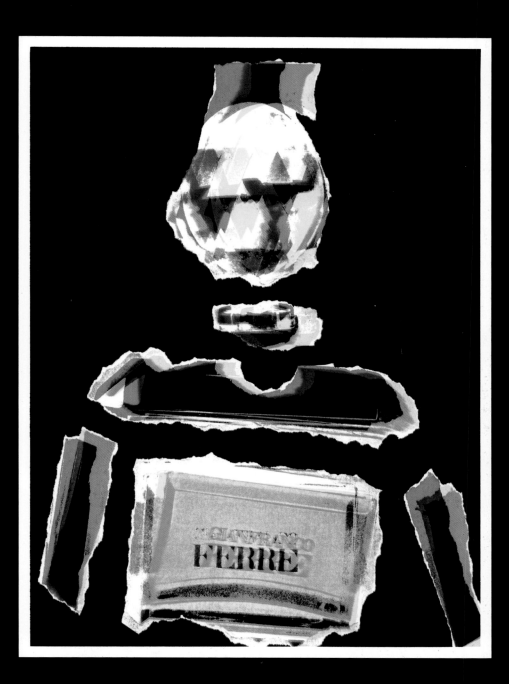

AVT/WINDOW*2:

AVT/SCREEN*2: 'SHOW's a FULL-MIX 'TRACK' with 'SAMPLE'd backdrop featuring monochrome 'SCRATCH'

AVT/3360

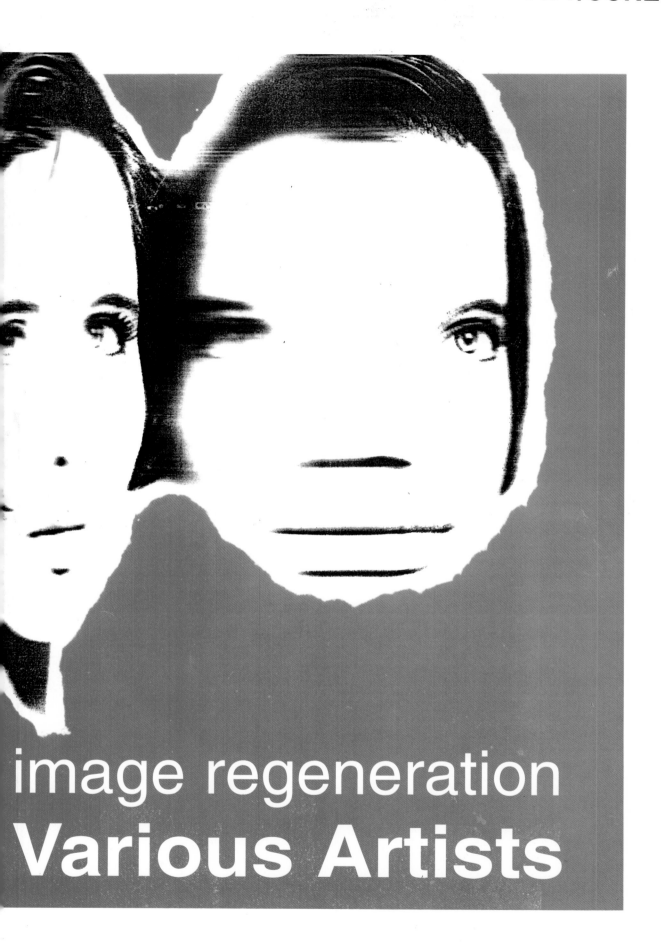

image regeneration
Various Artists

game over